BUSINESS QUOTES FROM WORLD BILLIONAIRES

Inspirational Vol. 1

I0470231

HENRY NKPADO

My Exceptionally Distinguished Mum

Mrs. Amaechi Mkpado

(The Greatest Woman on Planet Earth)

CONTENTS

ACKNOWLEDGMENTS

To the Prince of Peace, the Lord God Almighty who gave me life, and without whom, this book would not have been possible.

To My Master, Leader, Mentor, Father, Teacher Counselor, Role Model and Icon, His Grace, the Most Reverend Professor Daddy Hezekiah, Chancellor of Hezekiah University and Founder/Leader of Living Christ Mission. Without Daddy, I may not have been alive today and if alive, I may have derailed in all ramifications. I owe him the greatest gratitude

To my family (Mkpado family) and especially my beloved Mother, Mrs. Amaechi Mkpado, I salute you all. I will not fail to also thank Kelechi Mkpado for all his supports in my actualization of this piece. Specially recognized is Lieutenant Patricia Akubo for her patience, belief and supports to me. I am forever grateful.

To all my friends, colleagues and well-wishers especially Engr. Steve Onwubu, Rt. Hon. Jude Osuala and Eze Onuoha, I owe each and every one of you a huge debt of gratitude.

Finally, to the over 550 billionaires whom through various sources, I was able to gather cum compile their business quotes, I remain grateful for your words of wisdom.

1 INTRODUCTION

Putting together a book of this magnitude is not a tea party. It took me sleepless nights researching and writing out these great words of these distinguished business titans and captains of industries.

What then is the aim of this book? The answer is simple, it is to inspire you the reader to greatness: GREATNESS cannot be privatized; it is not an exclusive right of any one. Anybody can rise to unimaginable heights. It can be you! If these men can achieve it, you too can.

According to Oxfam in 2017, eight [8] men in the world today own the same wealth as the 3.6 billion people who make up the poorest half of humanity. Put differently, world's richest 1% gets 82% of the wealth. This truth is very scaring but any man or woman can aspire and achieve such feat. It is all about your idea, vision, hard work/smart work, creativity, boldness, challenging the status quo and sometimes swimming against the tides.

In the course of compiling these quotes, I discovered several reasons why we fail in business. It is only those that have succeeded that can tell you what it takes to succeed. Experience they say is a great teacher. Some of these top CEO and entrepreneurs have been in business spanning decades hence are in best position to advice startups and other business leader on the pit falls in business management and growth.

This book will challenge your mental faculty and ignite your passion to rise above the present challenges and impact your world. You are not too small to make a difference.

Inspiring quotes from notable business Icons and richest people on earth were adequately captured, cutting across different continents and countries including those who built their firm from scratch to unimaginable heights they occupy today.

Some of these exception individuals include but are not limited to: Jeff Bezos who is presently the richest man in the world, whose dad came into the USA as an immigrant. Others are: Richard Branson, Carlos Slim, Larry Page, Travis Kalanick (Uber CEO), Sir James Dyson, Sam Walton, Mark Zuckerberg, Aliko Dangote (the richest man in Africa) Elon Musk, Jack Ma, Amancio Ortega, Isabel Dos Santos Frank Iowy and many others (more than 550 billionaires).

I assure you that you cannot go through this piece and remain the same. You will discover several mistakes that made your business to remain where it is. As for startups or those still incubating their ideas, this book will give you the support needed to put things in proper perspective so as not to crash within a year of business startup as it is with several businesses.

Remember (for aspiring entrepreneurs) vision without execution, is just a hallucination according to Christiana Des Marais and knowledge without action is meaningless according to Abu Bakr. You must be bold, fearless and optimistic about your ideas and act. You can't predict tomorrow therefore put action to your idea. Someday it was Bill Gate, the other time it was Carlos Slim, today it is Jeff Bezos; tomorrow, it may be you! It is possible!

INSPIRATIONAL BUSINESS QUOTES

1. Building a business is not rocket science; it is about having a great idea and seeing it through with integrity - **Richard Branson**

2. If you are competitor focused, you have to wait until there is a competitor doing something. Being customer-focused allows you to be more pioneering - **Jeff Bezos**

3. In a world that's changing really quickly, the only strategy that is guaranteed to fail is not taking risks - **Mark Zuckerberg**

4. Your most unhappy customers are your greatest source of learning - **Bill Gates**

5. Competition makes you better, always makes you better, even if the competitor wins - **Carlos Slim**

6. In the business world, the rearview mirror is always clearer than the wind shield - **Warren Buffett**

7. We have been doing things that are contrary; the things that people tell us won't work from the beginning. In fact, the only way to get ahead is to find errors in the conventional wisdom - **Larry Ellison**

8. The role of business is to provide products and services that

make people's lives better – while using fewer resources and to act lawfully and with integrity and to act lawfully and with integrity - **Charles Koch**

9.   In the journey to success, tenacity of purpose is supreme - **Aliko Dangote**

10.   Being on entrepreneur isn't really about starting a business. It's a way of looking at the world: seeing opportunity where others see obstacles, taking risks when others take refuge. - **Michael Bloomberg**

11.   The balloons only have one life and the only way of finding out whether they work is to attempt to fly around the world. - **Richard Branson**

12.   It is often easier to make progress on mega-ambitions dreams-since no one else is crazy enough to do it, you have little competition. - **Larry Page**

13.   We don't like failures - **Bernard Arnault**

14.   There is only one boss. The customer and he can fire everybody in the company from the chairman on down, simply by spending his money somewhere else - **Sam Walton**

15.   The richest people in the world build networks; everyone else is trained to look for work. - **Robert Kiyosaki**

16.   The only way you finish with poverty is with jobs - **Carlos Slim**

17. I am not a person who pursues luxury. I am not like those people who, once they have money, compulsively squander it or show it off - **Wang Jianlin**

18. All my senior staff knows I demand efficiency. Before a meeting the other side knows what's going on and I know what they've done. Everybody is well prepared and no time should be wasted
-       **Kashing Li**

19. I am for maximum supervision and minimum regulation - **George Soros**

20. If you limit your goals to what you know you can achieve, you are setting the bar way too low **-Ray Dalio**

21. Customer needs have an unsettling way of not staying satisfied for very long.   -   **Theo Albrecht**

22. If you give me 85 billion today, I will invest everything here in Nigeria **- Aliko Dangote**

23. Some people dream of success .... While others wake up and work hard of it **- Mark Zuckerberg**

24. Brand is just a perception and perception will match reality over time. Sometimes it will be behind. But brand is simply and collective impression some have about a product **- Elon Musk**

25. Do one thing and do it well **- Jan Koum**

26. When the market goes to hell, it's more of an opportunity than a problem - **John Fredriksen**

27. People who just accept the status-quo and conventional wisdom don't make a difference in the world - **Eli Broad**

28. I am glad I am a property developer and not a historian because I make things and a historian only folks about things - **Harry Triguboft**

29. What makes eBay successful the real value and the real power at eBay is the community. It's the buyers and sellers coming together and forming a market place -   **Pierre Omidyar**

30. Our greatest weakness lies in giving up. The most certain way to succeed is always to try one more time. - **Thomas Edison**

31. People who dream small dreams continue to live as small people - **Robert Kiyosaki**

32. You are better off trying something and having it not work and learning from that than not doing anything at all - **Mark Zuckerberg**

33. It was almost as if i had a right to win. Thinking like that often seems to turn into sort of a self-fulfilling prophecy - **Sam Walton**

34. A year from now, you'll wish you had started today - **Karen Lamb**

35. The is no greater thing you can do with your life and your work than following your passions – in a way, that serves the world and you. - **Richard Brandson**

36. Every day we are saying "How can we keep this customer happy? How can we get ahead in innovation by doing this, because if we don't somebody else will. - **Bill Gates**

37. Swim upstream. Go the other way. Ignore the conventional wisdom. If everybody else is doing it one way, there's a good chance you can find your niche by going in exactly the opposite direction. Be prepared for a lot of folks to wave you down and tell you you're headed the wrong way. I guess in all my years what I heard more often than anything was a town of less than 50,000 population cannot support a discount store for a very long time. - **Sam Walton**

38. Remain close to government and a way from polities. It means deal more with the authorities and less with the individuals - **Wang Jianlin**

39. You got to build team that is so talented that they almost make you slightly uncomfortable - **Brain Chesky**

40. I am a man who keeps my word - **Masayoshi Son**

41. Serenity is pleasant but it lacks the ecstasy of achievement - **Estee Lander**

42. Remain true to yourself and your philosophy - **Giorgio Armani**

43. If people believe they share value with a company, they will stay loyal to the brand -   **Howard Schultz**

44. If you're not failing now and again, it's a sign you're not doing anything innovative   -   **Woody Allen**

45. Whether it's difficult or not, there will be a few people who are outstanding, who will rise above the rest. **- John Gokongwei**

46. One of the huge mistakes people make is that they try to force an interest on themselves.   You don't choose your passions your passions choose you   -   **Jeff Bezos**

47. It takes 20 years to build a reputation and five minutes to run it if you think about that, you'll do things differently. **- Warren Buffett**

48. Every time there's a crisis, we've gained a market share.   -   **Bernard Arnault**

49. You don't have to be a genius or a visionary or even a college graduate to be successful. You just need a framework and a dream   -   **Michael Dell**

50.   Some people get rich studying artificial intelligence. Me, I make money studying natural stupidity.   -   **Carl Icahn**

51. This is the problem of the world today. Nobody wants to take risks to risk being themselves.   -   **Giorgio Armani**

The Forbes World's richest man, Jeff Bezos. CEO Amazon. Net worth is 131billion US Dollars.

2nd Richest Man in the World, Bill Gate of Microsoft. Net worth is 96.5 Billion US Dollars

52.   People don't care about what you say. They care about what you build   -   **Mark Zuckerberg**

53.   Government caters to those screaming the loudest, regardless of what they're screaming about.   In business, its exactly that opposite. You invest more in the most successful departments and less in these that aren't performing. - **Michael Bloomberg**

54.   Optimism is important. You have to be a little silly about the goals you are going to set. There is a phrase I learned in college called, 'having a healthy disregard for the impossible', that is a really good phrase you should try to do things that most people would not do.   -   **Larry Page**

55.   Outstanding leaders go out of their way to boost the self-esteem of their personnel. If people believe in themselves, it's amazing what they can accomplish.   -   **Sam Walton**

56.   Japanese workers work harder, they have a stronger loyalty to the company and they tend to stay in the company for a very long time. -   **Masayoshi Son**

57.   Money is not my objective   -   **Desmond Sacco**

58.   The F-word here is focus   -   **Jan Koum**

59.   Always do your best. What you plant now you will harvest later -   **Og Mandino**

60.   To win big, you sometimes have to take big risk - **Bill Gates**

61.   The key is the internet. The United States is by far the most advanced country in this new digital culture, so we have to be

there. The internet is the heart of this new civilization and telecommunications are the nervous system or circulatory system. - **Carlos Slam**

62. The most important enjoyment for me is to work hard and to make more profit - **Kashing Li**

63. Making an investment decision is like formulating a scientific hypothesis and submitting it to a practical test. The main difference is that the hypothesis that underlies an investment decision is intended to make money and not to establish a universal valid generalization - **George Sores**

64. You cannot get into business for the fashion of it - **Azim Premji**

65. If you know how to select, you don't fire often - **Harry Triguboff**

66. Your future is created by what you do today, not tomorrow - **Robert Kiysaki**

67. To build a successful business, you must start small and dream big - **Aliko Dangote**

68. There are not many companies in China that dare to say in public, we don't offer bribes or companies that operate only by market rules - **Wang Jianlin**

69. If I'm going to invest in a company, I'm much interested in seeing who's there playing the management. - **Jorge Paulo**

70. Founders are like parents and the company's like a child -

Brain Chesky

71. The most important single thing is to focus obsessively on the customer.   Our goal is to be earth's most customer centric company.   -   **Jeff Bezos**

72. It's very important to like the people you work with, otherwise life and your job is gonna be quite miserable. -   **Elon Musk**

73. Risk taking is the cornerstone of empires   -   **Estee Lauder**

74. A lot of executives act like their time is worth more than anyone else's. But I always respect an employee who guards his or her time, even from me.   -   **Eli Broad**

75. Customer is king: King Never Bargains   -   **Anonymous**

76. Pressure can burst a pipe, but pressure also makes diamond - **Anonymous**

77. Learn from failure. If you are an entrepreneur and your first venture wasn't a success.   Welcome to the club - **Richard Branson**

78. I really had a lot of dreams when I was a kid and i think a great deal of that grew out of the fact that I had a chance to read a lot.   -   **Bill Gates**

79. If one of our customers comes into the store without a smile, I'll give them one of mine. -   **Sam Walton**

80. My parents made me believe I could do anything I wanted to do. They were really into empowering me - **Pierre Omidyar**

81. When I started, I had nothing - **Giorgio Armani**

82. When something has to be done, do it in France, we are full of good ideas but we rarely put them into practice. - **Bernard Arnault**

83. A brand is no longer what we tell the customer, it is what customers tell each other it is - **Scott Cook**

84. In the old world, you devoted 30% of your time to building a great service and 70% of your time to shouting about it. In the new world, that inverts

85. Do not watch that clock, do what it does keep going. - **Sam Levenson**

86. If you don't have room to fail, you don't have room to grow - **Jonathan Mildenhall**

87. Don't let people tell you your ideas won't work. If you're passionate about an idea that's stuck in your head, find a way to build it so you can prove to yourself that it doesn't work. - **Dennis Crowley**

88. If you don't understand the detail of your business, you are going to fail - **Jeff Bezos**

89. Our success has really been based on partnership from the very

beginning. **- Bill Gates**

90.   When I was very young, maybe 12 years, I began to make investments. **- Carlos Slim**

91.   I always know I was going to be rich. I don't think I ever doubted it for a minute. **- Warren Buffett**

92.   Cover the down side **- Richard Branson**

93.   Quality is the cornerstone of the Henderson Group underpinning all our activities. **- Lee Shan Kee**

94.   You can't be afraid to fail because that's when you learn   -
Michael Dell

95.   In life and business, there are two cardinal sins. The first is to act precipitously without thought and the second is to not act at all. - **Carl Icabn**

96.   If you just work on stuff that you like and you're passionate about. You don't have to have a master plan with how things will play out.   -   **Mark Zuckerberg**

97.   The goal as a company is to have customer service that is not just the best but legendary   -   **Sam Walton**

98.   I am a person who believes strongly in human assets, that is my priority -   **Jorge Paulo**

99.   I attribute my success to this: I never gave or took any excuse

-       **Florence Nightingale**

100. Think about your dream and have a stronger passion than anybody else. Then you will succeed in any dream that you have. -   **Masayoshi Son**

101. Business is there if you go after it   - **Estee Lauder**

102. Our team has always believed that neither cost and distance should ever prevent people from connection with their loved ones and won't rest until everyone everywhere is empowered with that opportunity   -   **Jan Koum**

103. Businessmen must move with the times. The correlation between knowledge and business as the key to success is closer than ever. -   **Kashing Li**

104. Excellence is a great starting point for any new organization but also an unending journey.   **Azim Premji**

105. No one ever made a million buck by being cautions or timid or reasonable. -   **Eli Broad**

106. It's been very gratifying to see that I was able to start from very low beginnings. -   **Harry Triguboff**

107. Success is a lousy teacher, it seduces smart people into thinking they can't lose -   **Bill Gates**

Third Richest man in the world, Warent Buffet of Berkshire Hathaway. net worth 82.5Billion US Dollars

Bernard Arnault. 4th Richest Man on earth. Net worth = 76Billion US Dollars

108. I think the simple rule of business is if you do the things that are easier first, then you can actually make a lot of progress. - **Mark Zuckerberg**

109. I must always try to do better because perfectionism and the need to always have new goals and achieve them is a state of mind that brings profound meaning to life. **- Giorgio Armani**

110. Find that thing you are super passionate about. -   **Mark Zuckerberg**

111. Almost everyone who has had an idea that's somewhat revolutionary on wildly successful was first told there are insane **- Larry Page**

112. You can make a lot of mistakes and still recover if you run an efficient operation. Or you can be brilliant and still go out of business if you're too inefficient   -   **Sam Walton**

113. At some point, you go from building the product, to phase two which is building the company, that builds the product. - **Brain Chesky**

114. I've missed more than 9000 shots in my career; I've lost almost 300 games; 26 times I have been entrusted to take the game winning shot and missed I've failed over and over and over again in my life. And that is why I succeeded -   **Michael Jordan**

115. The harder the conflict, the more glorious the triumph - **Thomas Paine**

116. The customer is not a morons, she is your wife **- David Ogilvy**

117. The biggest mistake is letting a mistake demoralize you -

Mark Zuckerberg

118. Money is not a goal. The goal is to make companies grow, develop, be competitive, be in different areas, be efficient to have a great human team inside the company -**Carlos Slim**

119. Lose your smile and lose your customers   - **Sam Walton**

120. The hardest thing to judge is what level of risk is safe   -
George Sores

121. Use money to make money. Save your first bucket of gold on small fortune-but then use it for investment. Don't just park money in the bank - **Lee Shau Kee**

122. When I started eBay, it was a hobby, an experiment to see if people could use the internet to empower through access to an efficient market. I actually wasn't thinking about it in terms of a social impact.   -   **Piere Omidyar**

123. Never say you cannot afford something. That is a poor man's attitude. Ask how to afford it. -**Robert Kiyosaki**

124. I enjoy myself a lot but I derive more joy in working. I believe in hard work and one of my business success secret is hard work. It's hard to see a youth that will go to bed by 2am and wake up by 5am. I don't rest until I achieve something.- **Aliko Dangote**

125. I've been in tankers for 50 years and I like it. For me, it's still fun. -   **John Fredriksen**

Aliko Dangote. Richest man in Africa. Worth 11.1 US Dollars

Mike Adenuga of Glo, 2nd Richest Man of Africa, worth 9billion US Dollars

126. Entrepreneurship is about turning what excites you in life into capital so that you can do more of it and move forward with it - **Richard Branson**

127. I have done industry, banking, insurance and telecommunication but helping children and adults is the project of my life   - **Olhman Benjelloun**

128. People work better when they know what the goal is and why. It is important that people look forward to coming to work in the morning and enjoy working.   -   **Elon Musk**

129. We've taken SMS technology for consumers and improved it. - **Jan Koum**

130. Someone once told me I'm a sore winner, and they're right I rarely take more than a moment to enjoy a success before I'm moving on and looking for the not challenge. - **Eli Broad**

131. Invention requires a long form willingness to be misunderstood. You do something that you genuinely believe in, that you have conviction about, but for a long period of time, well-meaning people may criticize that effort.   -   **Jeff Bezos**

132. Its fine to celebrate success, but it is more important to heed the lessons of failure.   -   **Bill Gates**

133. In the world of business, the people who are most successful are those who are doing what they love. - **Warren Buffett**

134. The two most important words I ever wrote were on that first war-mart sign satisfaction guaranteed. They're still up there and they have made all the difference. - **Sam Walton**

135. The point is you can't keep doing the same thing and expect it

to keep working   -   **Michael Dell**

136. There can be nothing without love. No money no power. Love is very important.   -   **Giargia Armani**

137. Our philosophy is that we care about people first -   **Mark Zuckerberg**

138. Chance favors the prepared mind.   The more you practice, luckier you become.   -   **Richard Branson**

139. Money is just a way of measuring whether the business is doing well or not, but money itself is not what fascinates me. - **Jorge Paulo Lemann**

140. You just need to come up with great ideas with passion, with a business plan and the money will chase you. - **Masayashi Son**

141. Touch your customer and you're halfway there.- **Estee Louder**

142. You miss 100% of the shots you don't take - **Wayne Gretzky**

143. The keys to brand success are self-definition, transparency, authenticity and accountability.   -   **Simon Mainwaring**

144. Everyone is not your customer   -   **Seth Godin**

145. If you aim of nothing, you will hit it every time. - **Zig Ziglar**

146. Keep your mental muscle loose, you have to keep stretching.   -   **Leslie Wexner**

147. Anyone who is not investing now is missing a tremendous opportunity. **-Carlos Slim**

148. To be a successful manager, attitude and ability are equally important ingredients. A leader inspires others to greatness. A boss dominates his subordinates and makes them feel small
    -       **Kashing Li**

149. Formula for success: rise early, work hard, strike oil
    -       **J. Paul Getty**

150. Don't go in and tell somebody else how to run their business.- **Carl Icahn**

151. Excellence endues and sustains. It goes beyond motivation into the realms of inspiration. **- Azim Premji**

152. Ebay's success as a company depends on the success of the community of Sellers   -   **Pierre Omidyar**

153. Chose the vision, not the money, the money will end up following you.   -   **Tony Hsieh**

154. As we look ahead into the next century, leaders will be those who empower others   -   **Bill Gates**

155. Your brand is what other people say about you when you're not in the room.   -   **Jeff Bezos**

156. Communicate everything you can to you associates. The more they know, the more they care. Once they care, there is no

stopping then.   -   **Sam Walton**

157. Think about it this way- if your company is like your child- a parent wants his child to outlive him or her.   -   **Brain Chesky**

158.   The most difficult thing is the decision to act, the rest is merely tenacity   -   **Amelia Earhort**

159. A lot of what I experienced growing up in the U.S.S.R and coming to the US as an immigrant actually reflects itself in whatsapp. Experiences from our youth shape what we do later in life   -   **Jan Koum**

160. When I look back at 50 years, I'm sure that the greatest achievement is that I have survived in the business and I have grown all the time.   Because it is obvious that it is a very difficult business and I managed to do it without going public or without having any partners.   -   **Harry Triguboff**

161. You may be disappointed if you fail but you are doomed if you don't try   -   **Beverly sills**

162. My goal was never to make Facebook cool. Am not a cool person -   **Mark Zuckerberg**

163. If you mess up, it's not your parents fault; so don't whine about your mistakes learn from them   -   **Bill Gates**

164. Vision is perhaps our greatest strength it has kept us alive to the power and continuity of thought through the centuries; it

makes us peer into the future and lends shape the unknown -
Li Ka Shing

165. I made 5127 prototypes of my vacuum before I got it right. There were 5126 failures. But I learned from each one that's how I come up with a solution   -   **James Dyson**

166. We are stubborn on vision. We are flexible on details   -
Jeff Bezos

167. An investor should act as though he had a lifetime decision cord with just twenty punches on it- **Warren Buffett**

168. Money and ownership alone aren't enough. Set high goals, encourage competition and then keep score - **Sam Walton**

169. You are not obligated to win. You're obligated to keep trying to do the best you can every day.   -   **Marian Wright**

170. I started the site when I was 19 I didn't know much about business back then   -   **Mark Zuckerberg**

171. Always deliver more than expected. - **Larry page**

172. People should pursue what they're passionate about. That will make them happier than pretty much anything else.   -
Elon Musk

173. First comes the shy wish, then you must have the heart to have the dream. Then, you work and work.   -   **Estee Lander**

174. There is no substitute for knowledge. To this day, I read three newspapers a day. It is impossible to read a paper without being exposed to ideas. And ideas-more than money-are the real currency for success.   -   **Eli Broad**

175 A goal is a dream with a deadline - **Napoleon Hill**

176. We all need to become more customer focused and recognize the power of marketing. -   **Nicky Oppenheimer**

177. If we are going to be part of the solution, we have to engage the problems.   -   **Majora Carter.**

178. If you can't tolerate critics, don't do anything new or interesting. -   **Jeff Bezos**

179. It is not an experiment if you know it's going to work.   -   **Jeff Bezos**

180. If you are in business, you are not enjoying, you are working.- **Jeff Bezos**

181. Regrets are born of paths never taken.   -   **Michael Dell**

182. Elegance should be a way of showcasing the personality   - **Eiorgio Armani**

183. No matter how small a project you work on and no matter what it is, put your heart and soul and sense of responsibility into it.   -   **Frank Gehry**

184. Inspiration doesn't respond to meeting requests. You can't schedule greatness.   -   **Jay Baer**

185. Fail often so you can succeed sooner.   -   **Tom Kelley**

186. Of my mental cycles, I devote maybe 10% to business thinking. Business isn't that complicated. I wouldn't want that on my business card.   -   **Bill Gates**

187. I built a conglomerate and emerged the richest black man in the world in 2008. But it didn't happen overnight. It took me 30 years to get to where I am today. -   **Aliko Dangote**

188. Business was like tennis. You don't win all the points and the sets but if you keep pushing and focusing, you can win overall.
-     **Jorge Pauls Lemann**

189. Entrepreneurship, you will only understand it if you experience it for yourself. It's not something I can explain in words   -
Masayoshi Son

190. I will continue to empower the youths that is my passion. The youths are the leaders of tomorrow. We must continue to support them.   -   **Jim Ovia**

191. We obviously try to be in tune with what our users want.   -
Jan Koum

192. Brand is just a perception and perception will match reality over time. -   **Elon Musk**

193. Show me someone without an ego, and I'll show you a loser -
Donald Trump

194. Share your profit with all your associates and treat them as partners. In turn, they will treat you as a partner and together you will all perform beyond your wildest expectations -
Sam Walton

195. The art of good management lies in the capacity to accept change and the ability to meld new and traditional thinking. -
Kashing Li

196. The CEO is by far the most important decision for a company. The company is going to rise and fall with the CEO   -
Carl Icahn

197. When hiring, if forced to choose between virtue and talent, choose virtue.   -   **Charles Koch**

198. I don't usually make political comments, because I am a business man, not a politician   -   **John Gokongwel**

199. Sight is what you see with your eyes, vision is what you see with your mind.   -   **Robert Kiyosaki**

200. Enjoy failure and learn from it. You can never learn from success.   -   **James Dyson**

201. People are the key to success or extraordinary success -
Azim Premji

Christiano Ronaldo, the richest footballer worth 450 Million US Dollar

Lionel Messi worth 400 Million US Dollar

202. On making their first hire –if we were successful, there were going to be a 1000 people just like him or her in the company.
    - **Brain Chesky**

203. Anything I do, I spend a lot of time. I do it with passion and

intensity. I want to be in charge.   - **Mark Zuckerberg**

204. Ideas don't come out fully formed. They only become clear as you work on them you just have to get stared. - **Mark Zuckerberg**

205. Definiteness of purpose is the starting point of all achievement -   **W. Clement stone**

206. Treat your customers like, they own you. Because they do   - **Mark Cuban**

207. Talk to successful entrepreneurs, learn about what they've experienced so you can avoid some of the pitfalls that come with wealth.   -   **Diane Hendricks**

208. Entrepreneurship without skill limits your growth potential - **Strive Masiyiwa**

209. Its very important for leaders in business to work to create human capital, a team that has the same sense of purpose and alignment. -   **Carlos Slim**

210. Diversification is protection against ignorance. It makes little sense if you know what you are doing.   - **Warren Buffett**

211. I wouldn't be where I am now if I didn't fail ..... The good, the bad, it's all part of the success equation.   -   **Mark Cuban**

212. As I grow older, I pay less attention to what men say. I just watch what they do.   -   **Andrew Carnegie**

213. Being in the consumer business helps us groom talent in areas like marketing, finance and logistics. We can bench mark our outsourcing business to our customer business and its best practices.   -   **Azim Premji**

214. I was building blocks of 8 units and now I'm building blocks of 80 floors high   -   **Harry Triguboff**

215. I always make sure I hire people smarter than me. - **Aliko Dangote**

216. To succeed in this world, you have to change all the time.   - **Sam Walton**

217. If you want to succeed, you should strike out on new paths rather than the worn paths of accepted success. -   **John David Rockefeller**

218. By questioning all the aspects of our business, we continuously inject improvement and innovation into our culture   - **Michael Dell**

219. Some people don't like change, but you need to embrace change if the alternative is disaster.   - **Elon Musk**

220. Trust your instincts.   - **Estee Lauder**

221. In some countries, whatsapp is like oxygen - **Jan Koum**

222. Winning isn't everything, but wanting to win is - **Vince Lombardi**

223. Don't find customers for your product find products for your customers. - **Seth Godin**

224. If you don't like something, change it. If you can't change it, change your attitude. Don't complain. - **Maya Angelon**

225. Money may be spent but never squandered. - **Kashing Li**

226. The most dangerous poison is the feeling of achievement the antidote is to, every evening, think what can be done better tomorrow. - **Ingvar Kamprad**

227. Its fine to celebrate success but it is more important to heed the lessons of failure - **Bill Gates**

228. Happiness is the secret ingredient for successful businesses if you have a happy company, it will be invincible. - **Richard Branson**

229. Develop success from failures. Discouragement and failure are two of the surest stepping stones to success - **Dale Carnegie**

230. I don't change my style, I allow it to evolve - **Gorgio Armani**

231. Treat and pay your staff exactly the way you'd want to be treated if you were in their place. - **John Paul Dejoria**

232. It's quite fun to do the impossible. - **Walt Disney**

233. You don't need a 100 person company to develop that idea. - **Jorge Paulo Lemann**

234. The greatest asset of a company is good people working together.   -   **Jan Koum**

235. I try to surround myself with people who disagree with me. Successful people tend to be very overconfident about what they know and it leads to tragic mistakes. That will not be the final chapter in my career.   -   **Ken Griffin**

236. We like to think of Uber as the cross between lifestyle and logistics where lifestyle is what you want and logistics is how you get it there - **Travis Kalanick**

237. I am a great believer in Indian entrepreneurship. There is a whole set of people doing so many exciting thing.- **Uday Kotak**

238. The most powerful element in advertising is the truth. - **William Bernbach**

239. A brand for a company is like a reputation for a person. You earn reputation by trying to do hard things well - **Jeff Bezos**

240. When we decide to do something, we do it quickly - **Carlos Slim**

241. What other people label or might try to call failure, I have learned is just God's way of pointing you in a new direction. - **Oprah Winfrey**

242. Everything I have is for sale except for my kids and possibly my wife   -**Carl Icahn**

243. Think big and don't listen to people who tell you it can't be

done. Life's too short to think small. - **Time Ferriss**

244. Success isn't about how much money you make but about the difference you make in people's lives - **Mark Zuckerberg**

245. Expenses should never exceed one per cent of our purchases - **Sam Walton**

246. The secret to successful hiring is this: look for the people who want to change the world - **Marc Renioff**

247. Don't kill competition. It is health for business. It keeps you the entrepreneur on your toes. - **Aliko Dangote**

248. Don't blame the marketing department, the buck stops with the Chief Executive. - **John D. Rockefeller**

249. You cannot get into business for the fashion of it. - **Azim Premji**

250. I interviewed the first 300 employees at AirBnB - **Brain Chesky**

251. The most common way people give up their power is by thinking they don't have any - **Alice Walker**

252. As a student, I had a hobby of inventing new ideas for products. For me, thinking of new businesses is like inventing new products. - **Masayoshi Son**

253. We set up a small bitcoin and elhereum mining operation ... that miraculously now is actually making a lot of money. -

Abigail Johnson

254. Success depends on employees. For me, knowing and connecting with my employees is very important.   -
Divine Ndhlukula

255. Tell me who your heroes are and I will tell you who you'll turn out to be   -   **Warren Buffett**

256. You cannot mandate philanthropy. It has to come from within and when it does, it is deeply satisfying.   -   **Azim Premji**

257. Investing in property is simpler, safer and far more straight forward and logical.   -   **Harry Tiguboff**

258. Managers will work for salary entrepreneurs create new businesses -   **John Gokongwei**

259. Anyone can become an expert at anything in six months, whether it is hydrodynamics for boats or cyclonic systems for vacuum cleaners. -   **James Dyson**

260. Sometimes your best investments are the ones you don't make.   -   **Donald Trump**

261. Always remember, your focus determines your reality. -
George Lucas

262. Shareholders need to have a real interest in the company they own. Too many are simply too busy – they are asleep at the wheel.   **Naguib Sawiris**

Francoise Meyer, world's richest woman with a net worth of 49.3Billion US Dollars

Billionaire Jacqueline Mars worth 23.9Billion US Dollars

263. I probably traveled and walked into more variety stores than anybody in America I am just trying to get ideas that will help

our company. Most of us don't invent ideas. We take the best ideas from someone else.   -   **Sam Walton**

264. I think people should be self-reliant. You should work and be self-sufficient.   -   **David Tepper**

265. In a recession, you must be able to call into question everything you've done before.   -   **Francois Henri Pinauit**

266. The most beautiful face in the world? It's yours. -   **Estee Louder**

267. Big shots are only little shots who keep shooting - **Christopher Morley**

268. Know your core competencies and focus on being great at them -   **Mark Cuban**

269. Every great dream begins with a dreamer. - **Harriet Tubman**

270. Life is too short to hang out with people who are not resourceful. - **Jeff Bezos**

271. A company needs a good infrastructure, good organization and good people if everyone works in concert then you can succeed.

-     **Kashing Li**

272. You should find an area that interest you and just get on the highway and it will lead you wherever you lead it.   - **Barry Diller**

273. If you are the CEO, you are the brand. -   **George Farris**

274. Start small and dream big   -   **Robert Kiyosaki**

275. The battles that count aren't the ones for gold medals. The struggles within yourself – the invisible, inevitable battles inside all of us – that's where it's all. -   **Jesse Owens**

276. Don't let anyone convince you that your dream, your vision to be an entrepreneur is something that you shouldn't do. What happens is that people who are well meaning, who really care for us, are afraid for us and talk us out of it. - **Cathy Hughes**

277. Choose the right employees and then set them loose   -   **Carlos Slim**

278. Celebrate your success and find human in your failures. Don't take yourself so seriously loosen up and everyone around you will loosen up. Have fun and always show enthusiasm when all else fails, put a costume and sing a silly song.   - **Sam Walton**

279. Recognize that there will be failures and acknowledge that there will be obstacles. But you will learn from your mistakes and the mistakes of others, for there is very little learning in success.   -   **Michael Dell**

280. Fast learners win   -   **Paulson John**

281. No one strategy is correct all the time   - **Paulson John**

282. I have only one idea, that is whatsapp and I am going to

continue to focus on that. I have no plans to build any other ideas.   -   **Jan Koum**

283. I focus on one thing and one thing only – that I trying to win as many championships as I can   -   **Kobe Bryant**

284. Think like a customer   -   **Paul Gillin**

285. The most important investment you can make is in yourself. - **Warren Buffett**

286. You have to manage money particularly with market economies. You may have a great product, but if your bottom line bust then that's it.   -   **Mukesh Ambani**

287. Anything I do, I spend a lot of time. I do it with passion and intensity. I want to be in charge.   -   **Eli Broad**

288. The more successful I become, the more I want to remain like me, with my defects and insecurities. -   **Giorgio Armani**

289. When a door closes, it you look long enough and hard enough, if you're strong enough, you'll find a window that opens   - **Jack Bogle**

290. Dream big and dare to fail   -   **Norman Vaughan**

291. Everything involves risk. No risk, no reward - **John Gokongwei**

292. It is said that to be an overnight success takes years of effort. So it has proved with me. -   **James Dyson**

293. If the customer loves you, the government will have to love you.
    - **Jack Ma**

294. Choose people better than oneself, train them, and challenge them. - **Jorge Paulo Lemann**

295. I believed that someday I would have a very big company, a global business and a very successful company -
    Masayeshi Son

296. Think about how much of an effort Coca-Cola makes to protect the recipe for coke. We have to do the same thing to protect our intellectual property - **Ken Griffin**

297. There are 100's of thousands of Uber partners and we are creating 150,000 jobs per month - **Travis Kalanick**

298. We are going to position ourselves as a world class financial institution. We want to do things that are comparable to the best in the world. At the same time, we want to have very strong human qualities. - **Uday Kotak**

299. Money coming in says I've made the right marketing decisions
    - **Adam Osborne**

300. You only live once, but if you do it right, once is enough -
    Mae West

301. Keep everybody guessing as to what next trick is going to be. Don't become too predictable. - **Sam Walton**

302. Don't think you are unstoppable or fool proof. Don't think that the only way your business will work is through perfection. Don't aim for perfection. Aim for success -   **Eike Batista**

303. I like winning. There's also a certain joy in it. I feel fulfilled by it.   -   **Carl Icoin**

304. In business, you invest when things are not in good shape. When you invest at these times, you take a better position than your competitors.   When there is a recession and your competition does not invest, they are giving you the advantage. -   **Carlos Slim**

305. I was a salesman in real-estate. I think I was a very bad salesman but I was a very good student. I learnt from my purchasers what they wanted.   -   **Harry Trigubott**

Kylie Jenner top Forbes richest young persons with worth of1Billion US Dollars

306. If you don't have ambition, you shouldn't be alive - **Aliko Dangote**

Alexandria and Katharina Anderson worth 1.4Billion US Dollar each

307. I know of nothing more despicable and pathetic than a man who devotes all the hours of the working day to the making of money for money's sake -   **John D. Rockefeller**

308. Change is something that is expected and therefore, not resisted   -   **Abigail Johnson**

309. Sooner or later, you will see a China based company that really has a global impact, and I think Baidu has a chance to become one. -   **Robin Li**

310. You can't do a good business with a bad person find the right people to work with and you can't go wrong   -   **Richard Branson**

311. The first step is to establish that something is possible; then probability will occur   -   **Elon Musk**

312. I can't worry about backward; I've got to look to the future.   -   **David Tepper**

313. If you don't sell, it's not the product that's wrong, it's you.   -   **Estee Lauder**

314. I know that if I failed I wouldn't regret that but I know that one thing I might regret is not trying   -   **Jeff Bezos**

315. Set your goals high: make friends with different kinds of people, enjoy simple pleasures. Stand on high ground; sit on level ground; walk on expensive ground. -   **Kashing Li**

316. I inherited the company from my father after he died very unexpectedly from a heart attack in 1966. He was just 51 years old and I was 21. -   **Azim Premji**

317. It's all possible and I'm living proof -   **Relph Lavren**

318. Shoot for the moon. Even if you miss you'll and among the stars   -   **Les Brown**

319. In business, you will be wrong by and large 50 percent of the time. The trick is to recognize when you have gone wrong and correct the damage – not to worry at the moment of making the decision whether it is the right one. -   **James Dyson**

320. I try to learn from the past but I plan for the future by focusing

exclusively on the present. That's where the fun is   -
Donald Trump

321. Do not be embarrassed by your failures learn from them and start again – **Richard Breson**

322. Capital is not scarce, vision is -   **Sam Walton**

323. Never ever compete on prices; instead compete on services   - **Jack Ma**

324. There is a job and then there is a calling. We want to hire people that aren't just looking for jobs; they're looking for a calling.   -   **Brain Chesky**

325. The best time to plant a tree was 20 years ago. The second best time is now   -   **Chinese Proverb**

326. Communication is not the very core of our society. That's what makes us human.   -   **Jan Koum**

327. You can't build a reputation on what you are going to do.   - **Henry Ford**

328. Passion is one great force that unleashes creativity, because if you're passionate about something, then you're more willing to take risks   -   **Yo Yo Ma**

329. I am the property of my business not the reverse **Amancio Ortage**

330. My courage in my own conviction was unshakable.   -
    Sheldon Adelson

331. If you think you can do a thing or think you can't do a thing,
    you're right.   -   **Henry Ford**

332. Ideas, more than money are really the currency for success. -
    Eli Broad

333. Marketing is too important to be left to the marketing
    department.-   **David Packard**

334. One of the great things about being willing to try new things
    and make mistakes keep you bumble. People who are humble
    learn more than people who are arrogant. - **Robert Kiyosaki**

335. Skills make you rich, not theories.   -   **Robert Kiyosaki**

336. All businesses make mistakes. The trick is to avoid large ones.
    -     **Carlos Slim**

337. You've got to take risks if you're going to succeed. I would much
    rather ask for forgiveness than permission - **Richard Branson**

338. Individuals don't win in business, teams do - **Sam Walton**

339. Focus is essential. You cannot be great at everything. We
    must concentrate on the essentials - **Jorge Paulo Lemann**

340. Have passion, have a dream for your own life, life is only one
    time -   **Masayoshi Son**

341. I still believe that sitting down and reading a book is the best way to really learn something. - **Eric Shmidt**

342. Many investors make the mistake of buying high and selling low while the exact opposite is the right strategy to outperform over the long term.   -   **John Paulson**

343. I didn't get there by wishing for it or hoping for it but by working for it   -   **Estee Lauder**

344. Investors who find the best businesses to put their money behind are rewarded for their research.   -   **Ken Griffin**

345. Every problem has a solution. You just have to be creative enough to find it. -   **Travis Kalanick**

346. The best customer service is if the customer doesn't need to call you, doesn't need to talk to you. it just works   - **Jeff Bezos**

347. Creative work gives you an almost indissoluble connection with people   -   **Giorgio Armani**

348. Don't take NO when your gut tells you YES" - **James Patterson**

349. Doing business without advertising is like working at a girl in the dark. You know what you are doing, but nobody else does.   -   **Steuart Henderson**

350. To be successful, the first thing you do is to fall in love with your work -   **Anonymous**

351. Dying rich has always struck me as dumb. There is still lots I want to accomplish ...and I have a number of philanthropic interests to support   -   **Charles Schowab**

352. Success can be achieved through hard work, frugality integrity, responsiveness to change, and most of all boldness to dream.   -   **John Gokongwei**

353. You've to make customers smart.   An e-commerce portal doesn't sell a product at cheaper rate; instead an offline shop sells it at costlier prices   -   **Jack Ma**

354. A lot of people died fighting tyranny. The least I can do is vote against it   -   **Carl Icain**

355. CEO's are paid for doing a terrible job. If the system wasn't so messed up, guys like me wouldn't make this kind of money.   -   **Carl Icain**

356. All my live, I've been winning -   **John Catsimatidis**

357. It's ok to have an egg in one basket as long as you control what happens to that basket -   **Elon Muak**

358. Over the past six years, I've had many difficulties. But I never lost my passion.   -   **Robin Li**

359. Our biggest mistake was not reclosing how illiquid markets could get so quickly   -   **David Tepper**

360. One of the big errors people are making right now is thinking

that old style businesses will be obsolete when actively they will be an important part of this new civilization. Some retail groups are introducing e-commerce and think that the bricks are no longer useful. But they will continue to be important
-     **Carlos Slim**

361. Somehow over the years people have gotten the impression that Walmart was just this great idea that turned into an overnight of everything like most overnight successes, it was about twenty years in the making.   -   **Sam Walton**

362. The most important thing is to build the best reputation   -
Kashing Li

363. I don't think that ambition should not be in the dictionary of entrepreneurs. But our ambition should be realistic. You have to realize that you can't do everything. -   **Mukesh Ambani**

364. Unless you pay the price for success, you will not know the worth   -   **Apoorve Dubey**

365. Manufacture, don't just trade. There is money in manufacturing even though it is capital intensive. To achieve a big break through, I had to start manufacturing the same product I was trading on; which is commodities -   **Aliko Dangote**

366. I always tried to turn every disaster into an opportunity   -
John D. Rockefeller

367. What happen inside the company eventually comes out – you can't hold it in.   -   **Brain Chesky**

368. You have to have a dream, whether big or small.   Then plan, focus, work hard and be very determined to achieve your goals   -   **Henry Sy**

369. I demand pretty aggressive goal setting and a commitment to measure progress towards those goals because I don't like surprises. I don't even like good surprises   -   **Abigail Johnson**

370. All great things begin with a vision a dream -   **Estee Lauder**

371. A lot of times, people start out with a lot of good ideas, but then they don't execute. They lose the purity of their vision. You end up running around in circles. -   **Tan Koum**

372. We cannot limit ourselves to continuing on the path we have already opened   -   **Amancio Ortega**

373. Competition commoditizes competency,   -   **Jay Baer**

374. Everybody can tell you the risk. An entrepreneur can see the reward   -   **Robert Kiyoski**

375. If you don't have time for the small things, you won't have time for the big things -   **Richard Branson**

376. Loyalty is not won by being first. It is won by being best   -   **Stefan Persson**

Richest Black Woman Folorunsho Alakija with a worth of 2.5 US Dollars

American media mogul Oprah Winfrey with worth of 2.5 US Dollars

377. I can't have my employees sitting in traffic when they should be

in the office. Spending two and half hours in the car is a huge waste of productive time.   -   **Azim Premji**

378.   Everything negative – pressure, challenges is all an opportunity for me to rise.   -   **Kobe Bryant**

379. I dress in my own 'Uniform' or my own dress code, which reflects my personal method and work ethic. - **Giorgio Arman**

380. You have to create something form nothing - **Ralph Lauren**

381. Opportunity lies in the place where the complaints are - **Jack Ma**

382. For things to happen in operations and marketing, you have to wear out the shoes.   -   **Jorge Paulo Lemann**

383. I am not a product of my circumstances. I am a product of my decision   -   **Stephen Covey**

384. Don't chase a girl, let the girl chase you. When you are shining, dreaming something big, the girl will chase you. - **Masayoshi Son**

385. Risk is what you make of it   -   **Ken Griffin**

386. Fortune favors the bold -   **Virgil**

387. I have got nothing against family companies, but there must be real equity, that is all I say. It cannot be based on influence or

political friendships. It has to be based on real equity backing their dreams.   -   **Uday Kotak**

388. If great content is the hero, then banners are the villains   -
Michael Brenner

389. Until you are ready to look foolish, you will never have the possibility of being great.   -   **Cher**

390. I've owned about 18 air planes over the years, and 1 have never bought one of them new   -   **Sam Walton**

391. Today I see a billion people as a billion potential customers, an opportunity to generate value for them and to make a return for myself.   -   **Mukesh Ambani**

392. For businesses to be successful, they need to constantly ask the question. How can we provide value to our customers? At the end of the day, that is what matters   -   **Eli Broad**

393. Your goal should never be starting a company. Focus on the change you want to make   -   **Mark Zuckerberg**

394. What you don't do is to surrender. You might retract occasionally, but you don't give up. -   **Chris Brogan**

395. If you don't drive your business, you will be driven out of business.   -   **B. C. Forbes**

396. You cannot have people in your organization who are pessimists. They take you to mediocrity.   -   **Carlos Slim**

397. Leaders always put their people before themselves. If you do that, your business will take care of itself - **Sam Walton**

398. The internet is the first thing that humanity has built that humanity doesn't understand, the largest experiment in anarchy that we have ever had. - **Eric Schmidt**

299. What makes innovative thinking happen? I think it's really a mindset. You have to decide. - **Elon Musk**

400. The internet population is going up and up. I am confident that this will be a huge market. - **Robin Li**

401. We don't really buy high flyer, we buy before they get high flyer - **David Tepper**

402. We won't stop until every single person on the planet has an affordable and reliable way to communicate with their friends and loved ones. - **Jan Koum**

403. I went through a lot of stuff to get to where I am - **Travis Kalanick**

404. Losers quit when they fail. Winners fail until they succeed. - **Robert Kiyosaki**

405. Our work is certainly challenging, but we are not under any pressure except for the pressure to outperform - **Kashing Li**

406. I formed an opinion that if I did things differently than the way everybody did it, that it would add value to every effort I made

-      **Sheldon Adelson**

407. If people are not laughing at your goals, your goals are too small.   -   **Azim Premji**

408. If I make money, I'm happy. Even if I lose money, I'm happy - **Lui Che Woo**

409. If you're afraid to fail, then you're probably going to fail   - **Kobe Bryant**

410. "And Si (Newhouse) who is a billionaire said "No, I'm not going to write a check for $1 million let's pay them $100,000 a month" and when I asked him why, he said, "I don't want them to think that money comes that easily. - **Larry Gagosian**

411. Every day is an occasion to reviving ourselves.   **-Ralph Lauren**

412. Train people well enough so that they can leave, treat them well enough so that they don't want to.   **Richard Branson**

413. Attempt to seduce the customer with the latest fashion, the finest design and the most attentive service. - **Amancio Ortega**

414. My job is to help more people have jobs   -   **Jack Ma**

415. My relationship with money is that it's a tool to be self-sufficient, but it's not something that is a part of who I am   - **Laurene Powell**

416. Brand is really the connection of you with your customers   -

Brain Chesky

417. I have never imagined attaining big success. Whatever I have achieved did not happen overnight, ever since my teen years I have devoted many, many years of my life to non-stop studying, diligent work and dreaming of a better future   **- Henry Sy**

418. You are only as successful as the people who work for you want you to be   -   **Leonard Lauder**

419. I loved retail from the beginning and I still love it today.   -
Sam Walton

420. A business has to be involving. It has to be fun, and it has to exercise your creative instincts.   -   **Richard Branson**

421. Frankly, I don't know how many companies there are, globally which are truly global.   -   **Azim Premji**

422. Experience, focus, smarts & desire make me successful   -
John Paulson

423. To create a big company, you need more partners, as it is hard to handle such project alone. Such projects bring access to the expertise and management resources of the partner and their connections above all.   -   **Vladimin Lisin**

424. It would be very hard for me to do things somebody else's way.   -   **Giorgio Armani**

425. Courage taught me that no matter how bad a crisis gets, any

sound investment will eventually pay off.   -   **Carlos Slim**

426. If you want Swash buckling action in your life, become an entrepreneur and give it a go. -   **Richard Branson**

427. Passion is what drives me forward; passion is what makes me go to bed at 2am and wake up at 6am   -   **Aliko Dangote**

428. Name, reputation and brand are invaluable assets that take decades to build and are lost in seconds - **Jorge Paulo Lemann**

429. I would rather earn 1% of a 100 people's efforts than 100% of my own efforts.   -   **John D Rockefeller**

430. If you don't take risks, you won't be able to do anything. I was confident I could use my experience to change and improve the way Macau worked.   -   **Lui Che Woo**

431. Ten steps to becoming a billionaire are: Have a successful father, Dabble in real estate, share the work load, acquire other skills, expand the portfolio, leave foot prints, diversify investments, harmony breeds prosperity, have faith in God, don't forget your roots. -   **Robert & Phillip N, Singapore Richest Duo**

432. No one doing big business can avoid some contact with government agencies, regulators and policy makers.   -   **Mikhail Prokhorou**

433. The best advice I could give to anyone is to spend your time working on whatever you are passionate about in life. -

Richard Branson

434. Whatever you can do or dream you can, begin it. Boldness has genius power and magic in it. -   **Johenn Woifgang**

435. I put $5 million into the real estate business when the world was coming to an end and three years later by 198, I woke up and was worth a hundred, that's a lot of money back then.
-    **John Catsimatidis**

436. I'm a man and I think every man wants to be No 1   -
Masayosh Son

437. Every day, you have to get up with new energy and new ideas to contribute to pushing the organization forward   -   **Abigail Johnson**

438. To achieve stable growth, an enterprise must live up to its conviction. -   **Cheng Yu Tung**

439. If you always think about your dreams or goals, work steadfastly towards them and continue to challenge yourself, you will definitely be able to realize those dreams or goals   -
Tadashi Yanai

440. There would be nothing more thrilling than to win a championship   -   **Stan Kroenke**

441. Never ever do business with the government. Be in love with them never marry them.   -   **Jack Ma**

442. I spoke to the 'wine spectator because that's PR, that's how you sell wine.   -   **Gerard Wertheimer**

443. If you are a big company, a big website, and lots of users come to your website, you will have attacks, and you have to deal with that it just cannot be a reason to take actions to exit certain markets.   -   **Robin Li**

444. I paid 1.9 billion in taxes in my lifetime   **- Thomas Peterffy**

Mukesh Ambani, richest man in Asia with a net worth of 53.2 Billion US Dollars

Mukesh Ambani, richest man in Asia with a net worth of 35.1Billion US Dollars

445. We keep our cool when others don't. The point is, market adapt, People adapt. Don't listen to all the crap out there. - **David Tepper**

446. I'd rather be a big fish in a specialized pond than a little fish in a more generalized pond. - **Leonard lauder**

447. Be simple and reliable - **Jan Koum**

448. I never aspired to be a public figure I have always been interested primarily in real business and the development of business strategies. - **Roman Abramovich**

449. Reputation is the key to success. You have to be loyal to your customers. - **Kashing Li**

450. In motivating people, you've got to engage their minds and their

hearts. I motivate people, I hope, by example and perhaps by excitement by having productive ideas to make others feel involved. - **Rupert Murdock**

451. When something is important enough, you do it even if the odds are not in your favour - **Elon Musk**

452. The secret of getting ahead is getting started - **Mark Twain**

453. My father begun to teach me about the business when I was about 12 years old that's when he first took me camping at the Kimberley's to actually see the iron ore country, appreciate its vastness, its importance and to teach me about minerals. He's still teaching me. The more I am with him, the more I learn. - **Gina Rinehart**

454. When we face our problems, they disappear. So learn from failure and let success be the silent incentive - **Carlos Slim**

455. The way management treat their associates is exactly how the associates will then treat the customers - **Sam Walton**

456. Essentially, whoever is successful, whoever is going to do things that make a difference is going to be talked about. - **Mukesh Ambani**

457. To do what you wanner, do to leave a mark in a way that you think is important and lasting – that's a life well lived - **Laurene Powel**

458. There's a number of things the CEO does but what you mostly

do is articulate the vision   -   **Brain Chesky**

459. I just want to be master of my own time. It is ironic that someone in the watch business should not be in control of his own time. -   **Jahann Rupert**

460. The rise of Google, the rise of Facebook, the rise of Apple, I think are proof that there is a place for computer science as something that solves problems that people face every day. -
Eric Schmidt

461. Authenticity is so important to us. -   **Sheldon Adelson**

462. You can never quit. Winners never quit and quitters never win
     -     **Ted Turner**

463. For a successful entrepreneur, it can mean extreme wealth. But with extreme wealth comes extreme responsibility. And the responsibility for me is to invest in creative new businesses, create jobs, employ people and to put money aside to tackle issues where we can make a difference.   -   **Richard Branson**

464. Our formats have opened 439 new stores during the year in which the landmark number of 3000 stores has been exceeded; with this respect; it must be pointed out that the opening of the store number 2000 took place merely two years ago and only six years have lapsed since the opening of our store number 1000.   -   **Amancio Ortepa**

465. Whether changes happen depends on people's mind and view.
    -    **Cheng Yu Tung**

466. Economics is about creating win-win situations. But in sports, someone loses.   -   **Stan Kroenke**

467. Luck is always the result of sweat. You have to work hard, but enjoy it.   -   **Jorge Paulo Lemann**

468. While recognizing your own weaknesses make the most of your strengths. I think this is the secret of success.   -
    Masayoshi Son

469. Not everything I do is purely for money of course, as a businessman and head of publicly listed companies, we have to earn, but at this point in my life, there are other considerations more important besides just money. -   **Henry SY**

470. We are in the business of selling pleasure we don't sell hand bags or haute couture. We sell dreams. -   **Gerard Wertheimer.**

471. Success is never final; failure is never fata; it is courage that counts – **Winston Churchill**

472. I am a believer in the journey and enjoying the journey – **Udak Kptak**

473. Social media are tolls. Real time is a mindset – **David Meerman**

474. The ability to sell is the number one skill in business. If you cannot sell, don't bother thinking about becoming a business

owner – Robert Kiyosaki

475. The more you know, the more prepared you will be when opportunity knocks. If you are lazy, and wile your time away, you would not know how to take advantage of opportunity even if they stared you in the face – **Kashing Li**

476. Love what you do or don't do it – **Mark Cuban**

477. I think the most important reason for our success is that very early in our quest into globalization, we invested in people – and we have done that consistently and particularly in the service business – **Azim Premji**

478. There are ways for fighting for your interest. I never do something in business that I wouldn't do in life. – **Vladmir Lisin**

479. Growth is never by mere chance, it is the result of forces working together – **James Cash Penney**

480. I'm not ashamed of being a girl, and since I'm a girl, I will do what a boy would have done had I been a boy. – **Gina Rinehart**

481. I learned from my father that you continue to invest and reinvest in your business including during crises – **Carlos Slim**

482. Nigeria is one of the best kept secrets – **Aliko Dangote**

483. Without internet, there would have been no Jack Ma and no ALibaba or Taobao – **Jack Ma**

484. I knew that I wanted to have a family but I knew that I wanted a career. I wanted it to be exciting, fast paced and challenging and something that would last for decades **– Abigail Johnson.**

485. If something is very important enough, you should try, even if the probable outcome is failure **– Elon Musk**

486. Fear is the disease. Hustle is the antidote **–Travis Kalanick**

487. The best way to engage honestly with the market place via twitter is to never use the words 'engage', honestly' or 'market play' – **Jeffery Zeldman**

488. Remember there is no such thing as an unrealistic goal – just unrealistic time failure **– Donald Trump**

489. Perseverance is failing nineteen times and succeeding the twentieth time **– Jude Andrew**

490. The best revenge is massive success **– Frank Sinatra**

491. Everything you've ever wanted is on the other side of fear – **George Addair**

492. Never bend the rules. You bend the rules a little bit, and then it's a slippery slope - **Thomas Peterffy**

493. I don't want to be the next Michael Jordan; I only want to be Kobe Bryant **– Kobe Bryant**

494. I don't have a formula to pass on; I always did it my own way.

Even today, I hold my independence close it is what is most precious to me. Passion. Risk tenacity, consistency. This is my professional history. **– Giorgio Armani**

495. No action is too small when it comes to changing the world . . . I's inspired every time I meet and entrepreneur who is succeeding against all odd **– Cyril Ramaphosa**

496. Investment are like trains and if you miss one, don't worry because another one will come down the line **– Charles Schwabs**

497. If your only goal is to become rich, you can never achieve it **– John D. Rockefeller**

498. Don't be afraid to win, do not be afraid to challenge. The goal is still **– Masayoshi Son**

499. The harder you work, the luckier you get **- Mike Adenuga**

500. High expectations are the key to everything **– Sam Walton**

CONCLUSION

There are many things to note and learn from this Volume one of Inspirational. First, there must be an **IDEA**. Anything that must be achieved begins with an idea. For those yet to start a business, the focus must be on idea. In getting an idea, you must think outside the box: What are the needs or problems in the society that you can solve? This is the bedrock of idea generation. You can also think of existing solutions to problems which you can re-create or rebrand. We can learn from UBER and many others, who reformed the transport system. A problem in the society can have several solutions. So if you can develop an idea into the millions of solutions to a problem, your noble solution can outsmart others and become king. In developing idea also, it is good to take cognizance of what your passion and talent really is. It goes a long way in making the business idea to stand the test of time. The genesis of Facebook as we know was not for business or money making venture, but passion. Today Facebook founder is among the first five richest people on earth.

Secondly, you must have a **DREAM**, a **VISION** and **MISSION**. Having a talent, passion or idea is not enough. Idea is the vehicle, but vision is the destination. It is the motivation that drives the idea. You must clearly develop a vision and a mission to back your great idea.

Thirdly, you must **GET STARTED**. The journey of a hundred miles begins with a step. You may never determine how the journey may be or how the end will be until you start. So get started.

Having kicked started the business; you now need **DETERMINATION** to push through. Expect failures, disappointments, heart breaks, wrong choices, harsh government policies but you must be tough and stubborn to your vision.

Once started, wear a lion heart and imagine that you have crossed a bridge and the bridge is broken. No going back, hence forward ever. Be patient. Nothing good comes easy. Starting a business is challenging; you will meet other competitors; you also need to make your own customers; recruit staff etc. So to succeed, patience, determination and focus are essential.

FINANCIAL MANAGEMENT AND DISCIPLINE is another aspect to be serious with. A penny or cent or naira is key and important as a million dollar or a million Naira. Careless and loosed spending is an introduction to business failure. This is why many businesses hardly last up to a year after set up. Business is primarily set up to make profit. As it progresses, there must be checks and balances if it is making profit or not and if not, re-strategize to start making profit. If it is making profit, it will be wise if you start saving as early as possible. Be careful not to be carried away by your early profits. Save or better still re-invest the profits. Be careful how you engage in social and humanitarian gestures in the early stages of your business. You must learn financial management and be thoroughly disciplined financially.

Next, you must leverage on **TECHNOLOGY**. No matter the sector of business you are in, you must embrace technology. Social media is the key into the future. Imagine, the richest man on earth makes his billion online – Jeff Bezos. What about Mark Zuckerberg, Bill Gates and several others who are using the internet and maximizing profits.

Another important point is the issue of your **EMPLOYEES**. Many businesses focus on their products or their customers with little attention to their employees. As a matter of fact, most of the billionaires as seen in their quotes, made their customers the number one, which is very important; but as advised by other billionaires, you must take care of your employees so that they can take care of your customers and your business. Employees are very significant. They can make or mar your business. Treat them as gold; pay them on time; see them as partner in progress and as a team, then it is automatic that they will treat the client's and customers appropriately and as desired.

Coming next after this is the way you treat your **CUSTOMERS**. No business is an island. The competition is hot outside and every business is developing strategies to attract the customers so you should make your business a customer-centric business. Treat the customers as the bedrock to your existence which is true. Treat them just beyond buying your product. Let empathy be part of the values of your business. Once there is conspiracy by your customer, that is, once they are dissatisfied, and exit, your business will definitely head to the rock. You must have a feedback mechanism to get information from them. You must study and know customers behavior. Only few customers will tell you when they are dissatisfied. Many will simply exit or stop patronizing you. There should be several channels to win the heart of the customers and retain them and hear from them for they are so important.

Finally, but not the least and which is the first, GOD ALMIGHTY is the bedrock of all achievements. I could remember reading through an interview granted to the riches woman in Africa, Mrs. Folorunsho Alakija, she expressed strongly, passionately and clearly that her success is simply due to the fact that she partnered with God hence, without God, she wouldn't have been where she is today. You may have applied all the strategies you know, have the best idea, have the best employee and be disciplined, determined and hardworking; if God is not with you, it would all end in frustration. Proverb 8: 18; Proverb 10:22; 1 Samuel 2: 7; Haggai 1: 6, 9 -11; Duet. 28: 20 are pointer to my expression.

It is my humble intention and prayer that via this compilation, businesses will be strengthened and new businesses will be born which will in turn create jobs and solve societal problems. See you at the top.

Thank you.

REFERENCES

Books

Books: Donald Trump and Robert Kiyosaki; Why we want you to be rich, Rich Publishing, Oct. 2006

Donald Trump, Think Like a Champion, Vanguard Press, 2009

Henry Nkpado, A Distinguished Administrator Par Excellence, Chmavin Press 2007

Internet Sources

Asad Meah, awakenthegreatnesswithin.com

Ventureafrica.com

Quotedragon.com

Brainquote.com

Exclusivemotivation.com

Quotewise.com

Joel Brown.addicted2success.com

A2quotes.com

Abram Brown. 75 Quotes on Business form Top American Entrepreneur, 2017

Ana Gotter, 105 powerful marketing quotes that will transform your business

Andrew Balckman, Top 40 Inspirational quotes of Black Entrepreneurs, 2018

John Rampton, 50 inspirational Entrepreneurs quotes 2014

Sam Walton, made in America, Batam 2012

www.forbes.com

ABOUT THE AUTHOR

Henry Chidi Nkpado is a graduate of Government and Public Administration from the prestigious Abia State University Nigeria. He is a native of Umuokpu in Nkwerre LGA of Imo State. He is an investor, entrepreneur and an author with two published books and some manuscripts yet to be published. He lives in Abuja, the Federal Capital Territory of Nigeria.

www.ingramcontent.com/pod-product-compliance
Lightning Source LLC
Chambersburg PA
CBHW020930180526
45163CB00007B/2960